CITY
mountains

CITY
mountains

John Parker

illustrated by
Elspeth Alix Batt

ASHTON SCHOLASTIC
AUCKLAND SYDNEY NEW YORK TORONTO LONDON

Published by Ashton Scholastic, 1995

Ashton Scholastic Ltd
Private Bag 94407, Greenmount, Auckland, New Zealand.

Ashton Scholastic Pty Ltd
PO Box 579, Gosford, NSW 2250, Australia.

Scholastic Inc
555 Broadway, New York, NY 10012-3999, USA.

Scholastic Canada Ltd
123 Newkirk Road, Richmond Hill, Ontario L4C 3G5, Canada.

Scholastic Publications Ltd
7-9 Pratt Street, London, NW1 0AE, England.

Text © John Parker, 1995
Illustrations © Elspeth Alix Batt, 1995
ISBN 1 86943 147 2

9 8 7 6 5 4 3 2 1   5 6 7 8 9 / 9

Edited by Penny Scown
Designed by Elspeth Alix Batt and Christine Dale
Typeset in 15/20 Casablanca
Printed in Hong Kong

CONTENTS

Introduction 3

Steel and Elevators 6

Building a Skyscraper 10

    Planning 10

    Below the ground 12

    Above the ground 14

    The core 17

Computers 20

Design 22

Glossary 26

Bibliography 27

Index 28

Introduction

Skyscrapers are city mountains.

They are the city's answer to
the problem of many people
and little land. Skyscrapers
make room for people by using
the space above the land.

A skyscraper is like a town in
the sky. It is made of steel,
glass and concrete.

Over fifty thousand people might use a skyscraper at the same time. It needs air, light, water, elevators and escalators, and may include restaurants, shops, gymnasiums, offices, a carpark, a movie theatre, a nightclub, open-air gardens, and a first-aid centre.

Skyscrapers also need safety systems, such as sprinklers, in case of fire or emergency.

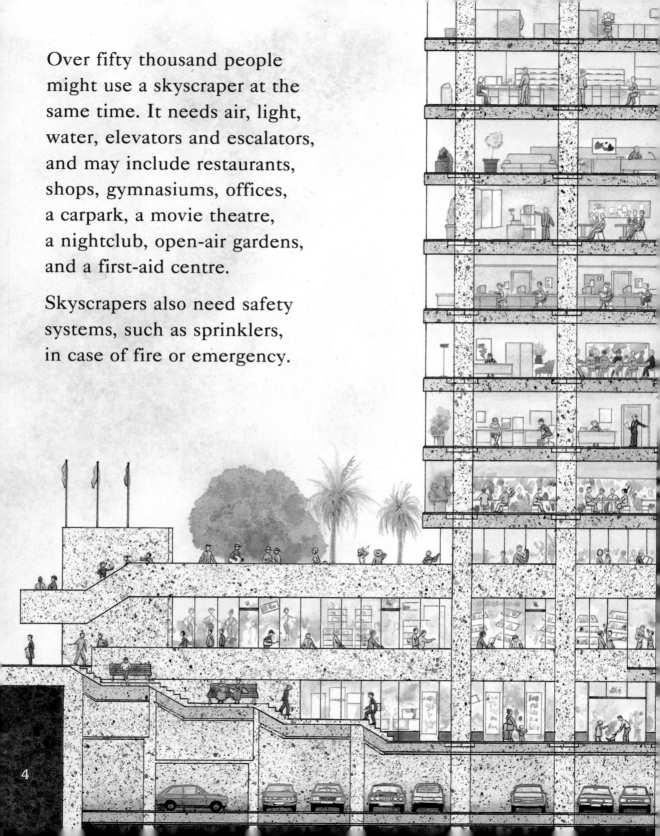

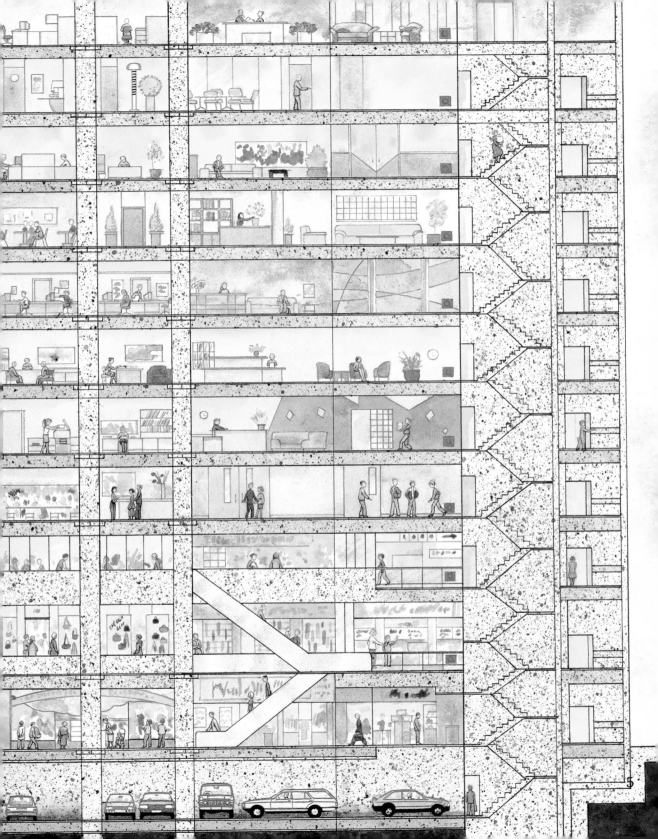

Steel and Elevators

In the middle of the nineteenth century, two inventions made the building of skyscrapers possible.

The first was the discovery by Henry Bessemer of a way to produce steel from iron on a large scale. Known as the Bessemer Process, steel is made by forcing air through molten iron in a very hot furnace. Steel is lighter and stronger than iron, and ideal for making skyscrapers.

The second invention was made by Elisha Otis. He invented the elevator, or lift.

Elevators made it easier for people to work in the top storeys of high buildings.

Nobody wanted to climb stairs all the way to the top of a building many storeys high. With the use of the Otis elevator, they no longer needed to.

Now, skyscrapers have many lift systems, as well as escalators (moving stairways), to move people quickly and safely.

The first steel skyscraper was built in New York in 1884. Only ten storeys high, it was soon overshadowed by higher and higher buildings.

The world's tallest skyscraper today towers 110 storeys (443 metres) into the sky. It, too, may be dwarfed by future super-buildings like the Sky City skyscraper proposed for Tokyo by Japanese builders – an awe-inspiring 1000 metres high.

Home Insurance Company of New York, Chicago, 1884. 10 storeys.

Flatiron Building, New York, 1902. 21 storeys.

Woolworth Building, New York, 1913. 60 storeys.

Empire State Building, New York, 1930. 102 storeys.

Sears Tower, Chicago, 1973. 110 storeys.

Home Insurance Company

Flatiron Building

110
Storeys

100
Storeys

90
Storeys

80
Storeys

70
Storeys

60
Storeys

50
Storeys

40
Storeys

30
Storeys

20
Storeys

10
Storeys

Woolworth
Building

Empire State
Building

Sears
Tower

Building a Skyscraper

Planning

Many people work together to build a skyscraper.

Architects make plans and models of the skyscraper. They also make hundreds of drawings for every part of the building. They test the model in a 'wind tunnel' to see if the skyscraper will remain strong and safe in high winds, and to ensure that it will not create strong winds at street level.

Architects and **engineers** need to know the weight of the empty building. This is called the **dead weight**. They also need to know the weight of the building with everything in it – the furnishings, equipment, and people who will use it. This is called the **live load**.

To make sure the skyscraper is strong and safe, engineers test the strength of the ground on the site. Then they and the architects decide how strong the base of the skyscraper has to be.

Below the ground

When all the planning is done, **surveyors** must measure and mark out the site before building begins.

Big, heavy machines such as excavators and bulldozers then get to work. They dig out the huge hole needed for the **foundations**, which are the parts of the skyscraper built below ground level. Sometimes they can be several storeys deep.

If the ground is not solid, **piles** are used. These are strong columns of concrete and steel, which reach down into the rock or more solid earth beneath.

Most skyscrapers rest on thick concrete slabs called **footings**, at the bottom of the huge hole. Usually the footings are on solid rock many metres below the soil, as they are in New York. Rock is an ideal base for skyscrapers.

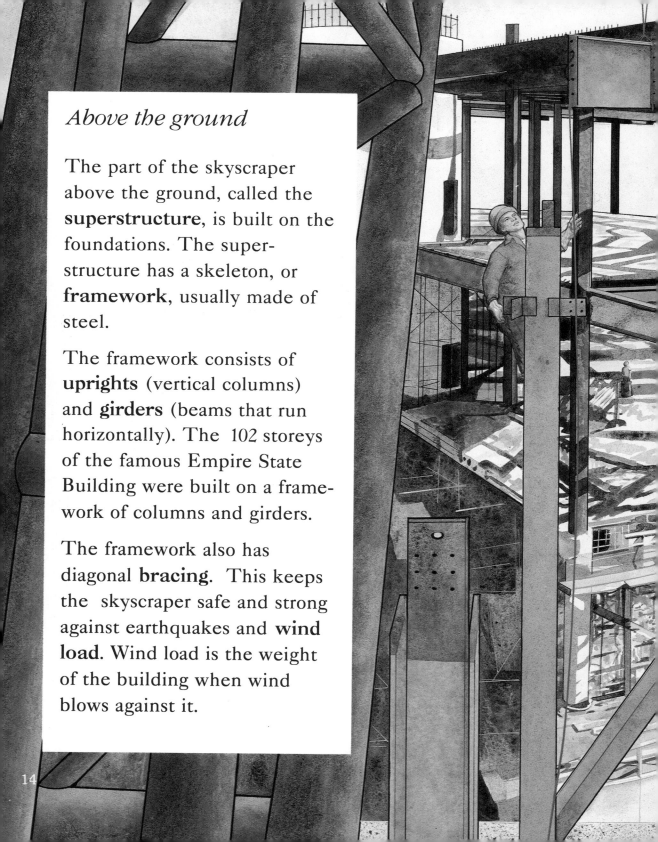

Above the ground

The part of the skyscraper above the ground, called the **superstructure**, is built on the foundations. The super-structure has a skeleton, or **framework**, usually made of steel.

The framework consists of **uprights** (vertical columns) and **girders** (beams that run horizontally). The 102 storeys of the famous Empire State Building were built on a frame-work of columns and girders.

The framework also has diagonal **bracing**. This keeps the skyscraper safe and strong against earthquakes and **wind load**. Wind load is the weight of the building when wind blows against it.

A skyscraper construction
site is busy and noisy.
There are bulldozers and
excavators, cranes, trucks,
materials, tools – and
many people who are
used to working high
above the ground.

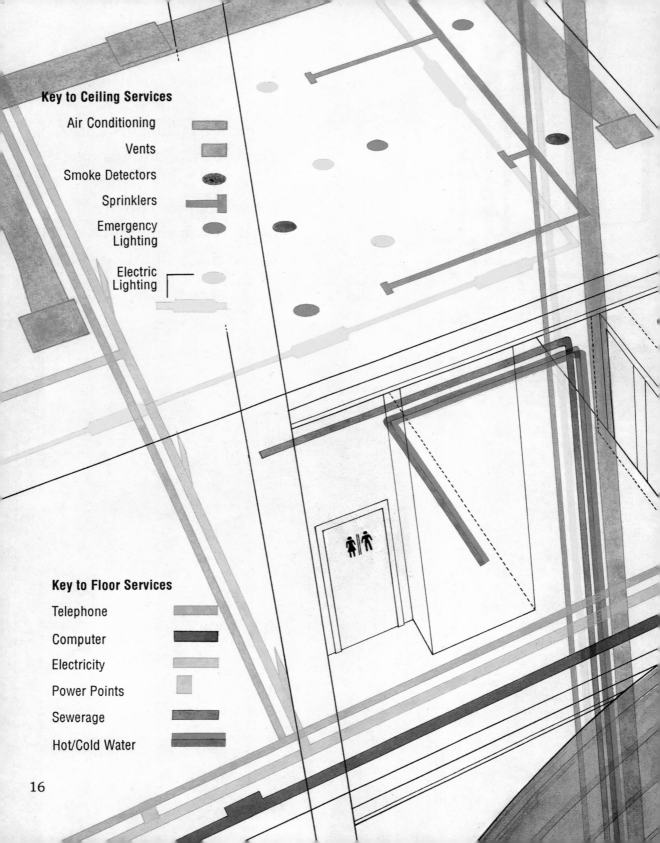

Key to Ceiling Services

Air Conditioning

Vents

Smoke Detectors

Sprinklers

Emergency Lighting

Electric Lighting

Key to Floor Services

Telephone

Computer

Electricity

Power Points

Sewerage

Hot/Cold Water

The core

The strongest part of the skyscraper is the **core**, which runs from top to bottom through the centre of the structure. If the frame is thought of as a skeleton, the core might be likened to the spine.

Inside the core are columns of fireproof walls made of concrete that has been reinforced with steel bars to keep it from stretching or squeezing. These columns carry goods and passenger elevators, toilets, stairs and storage areas.

The core also contains pipes, cables and wires that carry the services such as heating, air, electricity, water and lighting. These services are very important, and the ducts that carry them may be likened to the veins and arteries of the human body.

Sometimes the core is built first.

Using the fast **lift-slab method** of building skyscrapers, entire floors are built around the core at ground level. Cranes then lift the floors to the top of the core.

The lift-slab method almost builds the skyscraper from the top down!

Computers

The builders of the first skyscraper in Chicago had never even heard of computers. Nowadays, skyscraper builders always use computers to help them in planning and designing.

In many modern skyscrapers, computers are linked to hundreds of points throughout the building. Every minute of the day and night, they are checking to see that the heating, air and lighting services are running properly.

Computers are like skyscraper doctors!

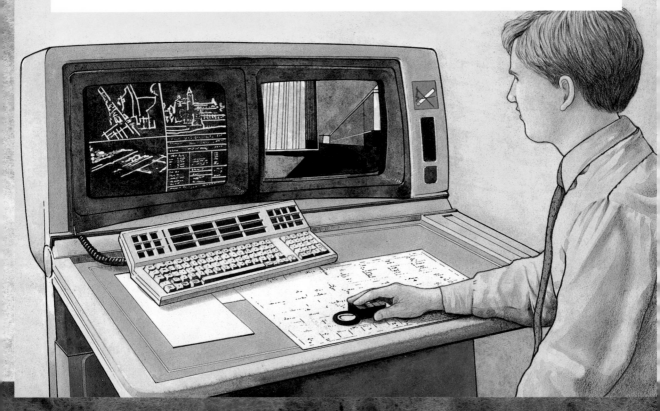

The Citicorp skyscraper in New York has a computer that controls a huge block of concrete lying on a slippery film of oil. The computer tells the block when to move if the wind blows too hard. These movements keep the skyscraper balanced and stable.

Without stabilizing devices like this, skyscrapers would sway and people might suffer motion sickness.

Design

The outer walls (cladding) of
early skyscrapers were built
in materials such as brick or
granite. They looked very
solid and strong. Since then,
architects and engineers have
discovered new ways of
building the exteriors.

Modern skyscrapers have their
outer walls built in **reinforced
concrete**, coloured glass, or
metal. These new, thinner
exteriors help skyscrapers
look light and airy and
also increase the
office space
for rent.

23

Glass-covered skyscrapers
sometimes seem to be floating
in the sky. At night, a city of
skyscrapers is a sky full of
floating lights.

They are the lights of the
city mountains.

25

Glossary

architect	a designer and planner of buildings
bracing	diagonal beams that stiffen the frame
core	the central, strongest part of a skyscraper
dead weight	the weight of a building, empty
engineer	a person who know what is needed to make bridges, roads and buildings safe and strong
exterior	the outside of a building
footings	the bottom part of the foundations
foundations	the part of a skyscraper under the ground
framework	the metal skeleton of a skyscraper
girder	a long horizontal beam, usually of steel
live load	the weight of a building, including people, equipment and furnishings
piles	strong columns, usually made of steel or concrete, that reach down into solid earth or rock.
reinforced concrete	concrete with steel bars running through it
site	the land where a building will be constructed
steel	a very strong metal made from iron
superstructure	the part of a building that is above the ground
surveyor	someone who measures and marks out building sites
upright	a long, vertical column, usually of steel
wind load	the weight of a building when the wind blows against it

Bibliography

Drexler, Arthur. *Transformations in Modern Architecture*, Secker and Warburg 1980.

Duncan, Michael. *How it is made – Skyscrapers*, Faber & Faber 1987.

How It Works No. 3, Marshall Cavendish Ltd 1974.

MacGregor, Anne & Scott. *Skyscrapers*, Pepper Press 1980.

Sabagh, Karl. *Skyscrapers – The Making of a Building*, Viking Penguin 1989.

Sandak, Cass R. *Skyscrapers*, Franklin Watts 1985.

Shaw, Peter. *New Zealand Architecture*, Hodder & Stoughton 1991.

Skyscrapers, Macdonald First Library, Macdonald Educational 1971.

Index

Bessemer Process, 6
Computers, 20
Core, 17-19
Dead weight, 10
Design, 10, 22
Elevators, 7
Foundations, 12-13
Framework, 14
Lift-slab construction, 18-19
Planning, 10-11
Otis, Elisha, 7
Services, 4, 17, 20
Skyscrapers
    Empire State Building, 8-9, 14
    Citicorp Skyscraper, 21
    Home Insurance Co. of New York, 8
    Woolworth Building, 8-9
    Flatiron Building, 8
    Sears Tower, 8-9
    Sky City, 8
Superstructure, 14
Wind
    stabilizing devices, 21
    tunnel, 10
    load, 14